CHOCOLATE CHIMPANZEES

By BLAKE HOENA

Illustrated by LUKE FLOWERS

Music Arranged and Produced by MARK OBLINGER

CANTATA
LEARNING

WWW.CANTATALEARNING.COM

CANTATA
LEARNING

Published by Cantata Learning
1710 Roe Crest Drive
North Mankato, MN 56003
www.cantatalearning.com

A note to educators and librarians from the publisher, Cantata Learning has provided the following data to assist in book processing and suggested use of Cantata Learning product.

Publisher's Cataloging-in-Publication Data
Prepared by Librarian Consultant: Ann-Marie Begnaud
Library of Congress Control Number: 2015958187
    Chocolate Chimpanzees
    Series: Read, Sing, Learn : Sound It Out!
    By Blake Hoena
    Illustrated by Luke Flowers
    Summary: A song about the ch letter blend.
    ISBN: 978-1-63290-589-5 (library binding/CD)
    ISBN: 978-1-63290-567-3 (paperback/CD)
Suggested Dewey and Subject Headings:
    Dewey: E FIC
    LCSH Subject Headings: Animals – Juvenile humor. | Animals – Songs and music – Texts. | Animals – Juvenile sound recordings. | Phonetics.
    Sears Subject Headings: Animals – Humor. | Phonetics. | School songbooks. | Children's songs. | World music.
    BISAC Subject Headings: JUVENILE FICTION / Animals / General. | JUVENILE FICTION / Stories in Verse. | JUVENILE FICTION / Humorous Stories.

Book design and art direction, Tim Palin Creative
Editorial direction, Flat Sole Studio
Music direction, Elizabeth Draper
Music arranged and produced by Mark Oblinger

Printed in the United States of America in North Mankato, Minnesota.
072016   0335CGF16

Take the letter C. Now add an H. Put them together, and what do you get? The CH sound! It lets us *ch*omp on *ch*ips or *ch*ase a *ch*ipmunk. The CH sound usually comes at the beginning or the end of a word.

The song in this book is *ch*ock-full of CH sounds. So turn the page and *ch*eer along!

5

See the chocolate chimpanzees
swinging through the cherry trees,
off to see their friend Charlie.

Singing chigetty chee,
  chigetty chee,
    chigetty chee chee chee.

Chuckling at a funny joke,
one their friend Charlie told,
about a chicken who crossed the road.

CHARLIE'S PLACE

Laughing chigetty chee,
chigetty chee,
chigetty chee chee chee.

The chicken had a bright red crest
and was looking for a treasure chest,
so the chimps joined her on a **quest**.

Chanting chigetty chee,
chigetty chee,
chigetty chee chee chee.

They chatted with a **chinchilla**,
lost at checkers to a **Chihuahua**,
and met a **charango**-playing cheetah.

CHINCHILI

BEST
CHIN
CHILI
IN THE
WORLD

12

Humming chigetty chee,
        chigetty chee,
                chigetty chee chee chee.

13

Then by chance they had some luck.
They spied Charlie the Chipmunk
with a treasure map hid in his **trunks**.

Giggling chigetty chee,
chigetty chee,
chigetty chee chee chee.

Charlie the Chipmunk jumped onto a train.
The chicken and the chimpanzees gave chase!

Chugga chugga choo choo!

Chugga chugga choo choo!

Chugga chugga chugga!

Under a chair and up a chimney,
down a slide and through a **prairie**,
they ran until their cheeks were rosy.

18

Singing chigetty chee,
chigetty chee,
chigetty chee chee chee.

19

When the chase was finally complete,
they opened a chest full of cheese.
They all cheered and began to eat,
Charlie the Chipmunk, the chicken,
and the chocolate chimpanzees.

Humming chigetty chee,
chigetty chee,
chigetty chee chee chee.

21

SONG LYRICS
Chocolate Chimpanzees

See the chocolate chimpanzees
swinging through the cherry trees,
off to see their friend Charlie.

Singing chigetty chee,
chigetty chee,
chigetty chee chee chee.

Chuckling at a funny joke,
one their friend Charlie told,
about a chicken who crossed the road.

Laughing chigetty chee,
chigetty chee,
chigetty chee chee chee.

The chicken had a bright red crest
and was looking for a treasure chest,
so the chimps joined her on a quest.

Chanting chigetty chee,
chigetty chee,
chigetty chee chee chee.

They chatted with a chinchilla,
lost at checkers to a Chihuahua,
and met a charango-playing cheetah.

Humming chigetty chee,
chigetty chee,
chigetty chee chee chee.

Then by chance they had some luck.
They spied Charlie the Chipmunk
with a treasure map hid in his trunks.

Giggling chigetty chee,
chigetty chee,
chigetty chee chee chee.

Charlie the Chipmunk jumped onto a train.
The chicken and the chimpanzees gave chase!

Chugga chugga choo choo!
Chugga chugga choo choo!
Chugga chugga chugga!

Under a chair and up a chimney,
down a slide and through a prairie,
they ran until their cheeks were rosy.

Singing chigetty chee,
chigetty chee,
chigetty chee chee chee.

When the chase was finally complete,
they opened a chest full of cheese.
They all cheered and began to eat,
Charlie the Chipmunk, the chicken,
and the chocolate chimpanzees.

Humming chigetty chee,
chigetty chee,
chigetty chee chee chee.

Chocolate Chimpanzees

World
Mark Oblinger

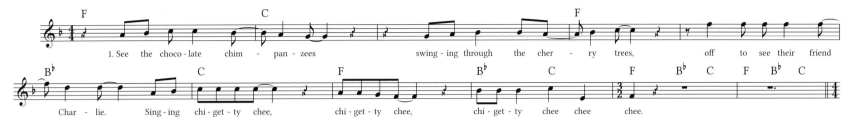

1. See the choco-late chim-pan-zees swing-ing through the cher-ry trees, off to see their friend Char-lie. Sing-ing chi-get-ty chee, chi-get-ty chee, chi-get-ty chee chee chee.

Verse 2
Chuckling at a funny joke, one their friend Charlie told,
about a chicken who crossed the road. Laughing chigetty chee,
chigetty chee, chigetty chee chee chee.

Verse 3
The chicken had a bright red crest and was looking for a treasure chest,
so the chimps joined her on a quest. Chanting chigetty chee,
chigetty chee, chigetty chee chee chee.

Verse 4
They chatted with a chinchilla, lost at checkers to a Chihuahua,
and met a charango-playing cheetah. Humming chigetty chee,
chigetty chee, chigetty chee chee chee.

Verse 5
Then by chance they had some luck. They spied Charlie the Chipmunk
with a treasure map hid in his trunks. Giggling chigetty chee,
chigetty chee, chigetty chee chee chee.

Bridge

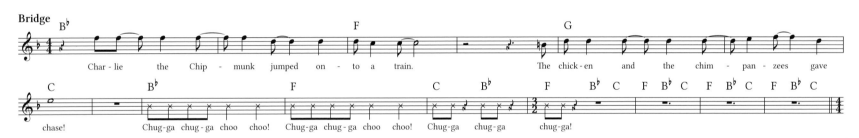

Char-lie the Chip-munk jumped on-to a train. The chick-en and the chim-pan-zees gave chase! Chug-ga chug-ga choo choo! Chug-ga chug-ga choo choo! Chug-ga chug-ga chug-ga!

Verse 6
Under a chair and up a chimney, down a slide and through a prairie,
they ran until their cheeks were rosy. Singing chigetty chee,
chigetty chee, chigetty chee chee chee.

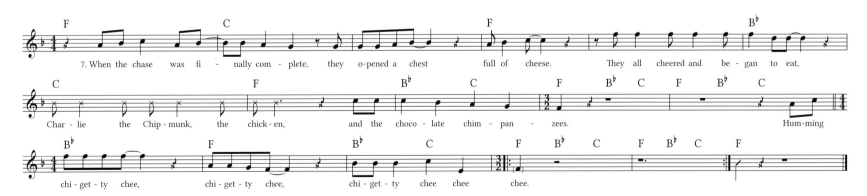

7. When the chase was fi-nally com-plete, they o-pened a chest full of cheese. They all cheered and be-gan to eat, Char-lie the Chip-munk, the chick-en, and the choco-late chim-pan-zees. Hum-ming chi-get-ty chee, chi-get-ty chee, chi-get-ty chee chee chee.

GLOSSARY

charango—a small Spanish guitar

Chihuahua (chuh-WOW-uh)—a small dog with short hair and big eyes

chinchilla—a mouse-like animal with gray hair from South America

chuckling—laughing softly

prairie—a large flat area with tall grass and wildflowers

quest—an adventure in search of something

trunks—pants

GUIDED READING ACTIVITIES

1. Write a C and an H anywhere on a blank sheet of paper. Then disguise the letters in a hidden picture. See if friends can find the C and H.

2. Go for a walk outside. How many things can you name that use a CH sound? Write them down on a sheet of paper.

3. Parts of the song have made-up CH words like chigetty chee and chugga choo. Make up some of your own CH words.

TO LEARN MORE

Mortensen, Lori. *Chicken Lily*. New York: Henry Holt and Company, 2016.

O'Brien, Lindsy J. *Chipmunks.* Mankato, MN : Creative Education, 2016.

Rix, Jamie. *The Last Chocolate Chip Cookie*. New York: Little Bee Books, 2015.

Rustad, Martha E. *Chimpanzees Are Awesome!* Mankato, MN: Capstone Press, 2015.